Interpersonal Skills

An Absolute Beginner's 20-Minute Quick Start Guide to Developing Interpersonal Skills for Work and for Home

Table of Contents

Introduction

With the aim of connecting you better with other people, this guide focuses on improving your interpersonal skills, so you can use these skills in developing stronger personal and professional relationships. It will aid you in assessing numerous people's interactions while providing you with the appropriate reactions and responses to each. In addition, this book will help you in forming new affairs and at the same time, assist you in preserving existing ones.

At the end of every chapter, there is a question that would help you assess yourself. Be sure to answer said queries honestly, so that you can truly determine which interpersonal skills you should work on and which ones you are already good at.

May these questions, as well as the whole book, serve as an instrumental guide for you in nourishing and strengthening your relationship with other people.

Thanks again for downloading this book, I hope you enjoy it!

Chapter 1 – Your Interpersonal Skills

John Donne was the English author who said the famous quote "No man is an island." His words meant that all humans are interconnected with each other and one cannot survive without the others. This quote from "Meditation XVII" perfectly emphasizes the use of our interpersonal skills.

To understand this concept, the question "What are interpersonal skills?" should first be answered

Interpersonal skills can be simply defined as the life skills that a person uses in conducting himself around other people. In simple terms, it is your ability to get along with others. The way you talk to other people, how you resolve conflicts with friends and colleagues and even how you participate in group activities all require the use of your interpersonal skills. Because they are part of your daily affairs or transactions, there is an essential need to continue in developing these skills.

It is a fact that everyone is born with interpersonal skills. All are capable of socializing with others. The difficulty in communication, however, lies in using such skills at the most appropriate situations. It is not impossible that you might have experienced a lot of awkward situations because you failed to properly communicate. Some people do, too. There are those who are too afraid to speak up in a large group or in a room full of audience. There are also those who missed their chances for opportunities because they were deemed "too shy" or "too reserved" to qualify.

Of course, there are also a lot of people who get misunderstood because of their choice of words. These are not peculiar scenarios. Although normal, these situations, however, could have been avoided had the people involved used the necessary interpersonal skills.

There are many interpersonal skills that a person has and can develop. The most commonly used are his verbal skills, non-verbal skills and listening skills because these are indispensable in both personal and professional relations. What skill you use and how you use it usually depends on different factors.

Sometimes, the nature of your work plays a crucial part. There are times when social standing or living standards become a factor, as well. Whatever you use your skills for, the constant reality is that they are important and you have to exert effort in developing them.

Chapter 2 – Improving your Interpersonal Skills

Now that you have an idea on what interpersonal skills are, you should then know the reasons why it is important for you to develop or improve them.

All humans have interpersonal skills that are not acquired through experience. Instead, some of these skills are innate within us. We have already acquired our skills when we were born and it is only up to us if we would like to develop them.

Most people work on their interpersonal skills through everyday experiences. To elaborate, people whose jobs require them to socialize have used their skills more than those who are usually isolated from other people. Scientific researchers, being mostly confined to their laboratories, are not as sociable as those who are in the sales or public relations industry, who always need to converse with other people such as their clients or suppliers. That being said, work or employment is one of the best reasons why you should work on your interpersonal skills better.

Most companies today are looking for employees with pleasing personalities and what better way to meet such standards than to work on your interpersonal skills. Improving your communication skills, both verbally and non-verbally will be a good start. Take into mind that a good employee does not just deliver good results, but he is able to communicate effectively as well.

Of course, if your verbal and non-verbal skills are coupled with your organization skills, employers would be greatly impressed because you have a holistic approach with work. Furthermore, having good interpersonal skills enable you to form harmonious relationships with your colleagues. A good working relationship will be greatly beneficial in the long run.

Many people fail to realize the importance of working well with other people. However, this should not be the norm. Instead, it should be remembered that one's progress or advancement would also have to depend on his or her social skills at work. It has been said a lot of times that no matter how good one is as a professional, a part of his promotion in the company will have to rely on how he is able to work efficiently with others. To avoid this dilemma, be sure to socialize with your co-workers.

Another reason to improve your interpersonal skills is that it can serve as a good foundation for both creating and preserving personal relationships. Forming relationships is quite difficult to do if you are, by nature, a timid person. However, this does not mean that you can no longer start or maintain relationships. Many interpersonal skills can help you work on your affairs even if you are not exactly expressive. The best skill that you should work on is your non-verbal communication skills.

Although you may not be able to express yourself successfully through words, through non-verbal communication skills, you can convey your feelings or intentions. Aside from forming and preserving your relationships, your interpersonal skills are also essential in mending broken affairs. You can fix many situations by a mere hug, by a helping hand or even by just lending an ear.

Lastly, having good interpersonal skills can also develop you as a person. If you use your skills to form good relationships both at work and at home, you will definitely feel a sense of fulfillment as a social being.

Chapter 3 – Verbal Communication Skills: Your Way with Words

Verbal communication is not just what you say when you are talking to other people, but it is also how you actually deliver your words. When you were younger, you were consistently told to not "eat your words" when talking. Although it was quite difficult to comprehend what that meant at the time, you should now understand that it means to speak as clearly as possible.

For verbal communication skills, there are three C's that you must take note of: Clarity, Composure and Confidence.

1. Clarity is considered the most effective factor in having excellent verbal communication skills. Many people fail in communicating with others because they do not exert a lot of effort in this area. Clarity as to communication means that you are able to express your words in a clear and precise manner. There is clarity when the person you are talking to successfully understood your words and was able to get the idea behind your message. Thus, people who speak silently or those who speak hastily most likely do not produce a clear conversation. Do not make the same mistake.

After composing your thoughts, take the necessary time to speak out your words so that you can avoid misunderstandings or misinterpretations. Furthermore, learn to stop when the situation or conversation calls for it. It is very common nowadays to have misunderstandings because people no longer feel the need to pause once in a while. However, you cannot entirely blame these people. The world today is fast paced and people are always on the go. Nevertheless, when you are facing important circumstances that call for wise answers, it is best to stop and think first and then answer intelligently.

2. The second C of verbal communication skills is composure. Composure means that you are able to deliver your words well because you composed them according to the situation on hand. Composed people are always polite and they do not have an annoying tone in their voice whenever they talk to others. Some do this because they feel superior over the others or because they do not respect the other person they are talking to. Do not do this. When speaking with others, it is important to maintain a polite and calm tone. This is important regardless of who you are talking to.

3. Lastly, in developing your interpersonal skills, always work on your confidence. People who are confident with how they speak rarely have trouble in getting their messages across. Of course, being confident does not mean that you just speak well. More than that, you should be confident because you know what you are speaking of.

   Some people have the tendency to bluff their way in situations. As long as they can project that they know the subject matter, they could get away with it. Do not be one of those people. Do not be pretentious. Instead, learn the topic on hand and converse accordingly.

When evaluating your verbal communication skills, the question you should ponder on is "Do people understand my words based on how I intend them to be?" If yes, then you have effective verbal communication skills. If not, then you should work on this area more by instilling the three C's in your everyday affairs.

Chapter 4 – Nonverbal Communication Skills: Your Body Language

There are many things that words cannot express and this is where your non-verbal communication skills come in. True to the saying "actions speak louder than words", the effect that gestures make is proven to be more significant to everyone, personally and professionally. There have been countless times when an "I care for you" note is considered sweet, but the warmth of holding another person's hand is sweeter.

At work, acknowledging your assistant's hard work with a pat in the back or through a congratulatory handshake is actually more relieving than a "Good job" card. However, communicating with gestures is not always advantageous. There is always a high possibility that one will be misunderstood when he uses non-verbal actions so it is important to be cautious.

You can express your non-verbal communication skills through voice, posture, gestures or through your facial expressions.

The kind of tone that you use in your voice sometimes speaks more than the words you actually say so be sure that you always consider this. There are times when you may be so caught up with your own stresses and problems that you fail to notice that you are already raising your voice. Although quite understandable, this is something that you should avoid. No matter who you are talking to, always speak in a reasonable tone. Whether you are giving orders to a subordinate or explaining a tricky subject to a little child, consider what tone you are using.

Of course, if you need to regulate your voice when criticizing someone, you also need to consider the same when speaking with affection. It has been scientifically proven that warm words, when spoken with a sweet voice, are accepted better and contribute a lot to a person's current emotions. Therefore, the next time you want to encourage or comfort a friend, be reminded that the right words will not suffice if given without even a hint of emotion.

Another source of your non-verbal communication skills is through your posture and most people tend to neglect the effect that their body language has. If you slack on your seat during an important meeting, the other person would have an impression that you are not interested in the conversation. If you constantly tap your feet when talking to someone, there is a presumption that you would rather be in a different place.

It is important to be careful with your posture because although subtle, they nevertheless send some strong signals to the person you are talking to. Make it a point to work on your posture. Always be conscious about what kind of impression you are giving.

Your gestures, no matter how simple, can cultivate your relationships tremendously. A small act of kindness can do a lot. Dropping off a coffee and snacks for a stressed out sister will surely boost both her spirit and your relationship. A loved one will surely appreciate a comforting massage after a tiring day. A thoughtful child who prepared breakfast for his mother will surely be appreciated.

A sweet gesture is always cherished, especially during times when they are least expected. When you perform gestures, it does not just say about how you value your relationship with that other person, but it also says a lot about how important he is to you. When you make someone feel important, it will surely improve your relationship.

Using different facial expressions is one of the most effective ways to communicate without words. A frown will clearly manifest disappointment or sadness. A tensed face will show anxiety or nervousness. A smile always brightens up other people's days. Facial expressions say a lot so you should never underestimate its ability to communicate with other people.

When evaluating your non-verbal communication skills, the question you should ponder on is this: "Do my actions accurately portray my intentions?" If your actions are well received and are responded to by others correctly, then your non-verbal communication skills are effective. However, if you are commonly misunderstood, then it is best to assess what kind of impression your actions are making and work on improving them.

Chapter 5 – Listening Skill: Shut up and Listen

It has been widely observed that most people only listen so they can respond and not to fully understand the message that they are getting. At one point, we are all guilty of doing this. However, this is actually the norm. This is because as humans, we are used to having a subsequent and instant reaction to every situation.

It is important to listen and to do it intently. You might have experienced being caught off guard by someone else during a conversation because you were not listening well. You may have been embarrassed in class when your teacher called on you and you were not able to answer because your mind was wandering off. You may have, at one time, gave a non-responsive answer to a question because you did not let the other person finish. These are just some of the scenarios that happen because you have failed to listen.

Being a sociable person does not always mean that you are always the "giving end" of the conversation or the one who always has something to say. It also means that you are a good listener because communication goes both ways. Speaking and listening make up for good and effective communication. By speaking, you get your ideas across. By listening, you gather another person's ideas. However, how can you exactly interpret his ideas and his message if you failed to understand? How can you respond appropriately if you were not listening?

When you are conversing with other people, try to look them in the eyes so that you can really focus on them and on what they say. Based on research, when you are looking at the other person's eyes while he is talking, the tendency is you would not get distracted with other things. Also, try to avoid unnecessary sources of interruptions when in the middle of a conversation. For instance, if you are in an important meeting, turn off your mobile phones or hide it from your view so that you would not be tempted to check it every now and then.

It is important to show the other person that you are listening because this is a sign of respect. However, on the more sensitive side of things, when you listen, you also show that you are very interested in what the other person is saying. Mostly crucial in personal relationships, you must use your listening skill properly so that the other person can feel that you are definitely devoted to your conversation. At the same time, when you listen, it shows that you consider him important enough because you have afforded him your undivided attention.

When evaluating your listening skills, you should ask yourself this question: "Did I hear or did I listen?" Hearing means you have made sense of the sounds, but listening means you have made sense of the words. If you only heard what the other person is saying, then you have not fully made use of your listening skills. You should improve more on this area by learning how to focus during conversations. However, if you were able to interpret his words correctly and you responded appropriately, then you have used your listening skills well.

Chapter 6 – Decision Making Skills: Ensuring Done Deals

There are always situations wherein you will have trouble deciding. Sometimes, the pressure gets into you and you end up relaying the task to another person. This really happens and you should avoid it as much as possible.

This chapter deals with your ability to explore different options given to you, and how you decide and how you abide by your own decisions.

The number one reason why you should improve your decision-making skills is that you do not want to create a bad impression. Others do not fully rely upon people who fail to develop their decision-making. Because of their inability to decide, these people are not depended on with high-profile cases or huge responsibilities at work. Fearing that they might make an unwise decision or that they would just delegate the work to someone else, bosses of these kinds of people doubt their employees and their capacity to work effectively. Do not let this happen to you.

If you want to avoid this kind of situation, you should then work on your decision-making skills. It is a fact that decisions are always difficult to reach because they come with their necessary and sometimes unwanted, consequences. However, you should accept the reality that decisions are part of life and you need to make them whether you like it or not.

To help you improve your decision-making skills, you should follow these three steps:

1. Assess the situation thoroughly.

The primary reason why you are given the task to decide on matters is that there is an underlying conflict that needs to be worked on. When said situations arise, the first thing you should do is to evaluate the problem thoroughly. Study every point and assess your possible options. The best way to decide is by knowing which choice is the right one so you should always make sure that you have all the possible options that the present situation can offer.

2. Make a decision.

After studying the situation, you have to make a decision. There are no perfect decisions as there might be consequences that may not be favorable to you or to others. The most practical thing to do is to consider every factor and decide which among these choices would be the least prejudicial to you.

3. Abide by your decision

As mentioned earlier, there is no seamless decision so there is a possibility that people will question your choices. This is very normal and it should not falter your self-confidence. Instead, continue to abide by your decision and defend it. Always remember that although there are no perfect decisions, there are still wise ones. You can only make this kind of decision through your effective and efficient decision-making skills.

The question you should ask yourself when evaluating this skill is this: "Do I make my decisions or do the decisions make me?" If it is the former, then you have good decision-making skills because you are able to control the situation and you deal with it according to your assessments. However, if it is the latter, you should go through the three steps once again and keep working on your skills until you have mastered the art of deciding wisely.

Chapter 7 - Negotiation Skills: Finding a Common Ground with Others

All people are born with negotiation skills, but not everyone knows how to use them well. Many people easily give up on a situation because they are afraid to discuss matters. Some people also lose disputes because they do not stand firm with their arguments. There are also a lot of people who get swayed easily by persuasive opinions because they fail to point out theirs. At all costs, do not let this happen to you.

When you are in the middle of a tricky dilemma, always evaluate if negotiation is possible. If it is, then try to compromise with the other party so that you can discuss different solutions. Listen to the other person's side and do not reject his views right away.

When it is your turn to speak up, explain yourself well without sounding superior. Be sure to communicate your ideas properly and respectfully. Stick to the goal of finding a common ground, even if it is quite difficult to do.

The reason why the negotiation skill is important is that it helps people agree on matters that are quite difficult to settle on. There are always different sides to every situation and through negotiations, it is possible to avoid conflicts and properly reach agreements. This skill is particularly helpful for lawyers and businessmen.

When working with your negotiating skills, you must ask yourself this question: "Was the agreement reached in the middle, with no losing party?" If yes, then you have successfully negotiated with another person. If not, then your skills were not sufficient to reach an agreement and you will need to practice your persuasive qualities more.

Chapter 8 – Assertion Skills: Respect Begets Respect

Some people have the tendency to avoid conflicts. Afraid of straining relationships, they would just rather keep quiet than air out their opinions or preferences. A good communicator does not do this.

Being assertive does not have to mean that you will be stubborn. It only means that you recognize your rights and that you are willing to fight for them. As rational beings, we all have different reasons for our actions. Some of our reasons will be difficult to harmonize with other people's reasons. Thus, conflicts will arise. While it is very much encouraged that you get along with others through the help of your other interpersonal skills, it is also highly advised that you work hard on your assertion skills as well.

Being able to get along with others does not mean that you should just give in to their demands. Said situation does not create a relationship of mutual respect. To have an effective relationship with others, you should be able to voice out your rights, without the fear of offending the others. You, as an individual, are entitled to your rights and it is only up to you to assert them accordingly.

Do not be afraid to stand up for yourself. Do not let others walk on you just because you do not want to create ill relationships. If you believe you have a right, then stand up for it. Do not be a pushover.

However, it is important to not just say what your side of the matter is. It is also equally important to know how to express your side or opinions properly and politely. The manner of delivering is as important as what you are supposed to deliver. Respect other people's views, even if they contradict yours. If you have to oppose it, then do it in a pleasant and humble manner.

The question to ask yourself when evaluating your assertiveness is "Do I communicate my rights politely and effectively?" If you answer yes to this question, then you have no trouble with this particular interpersonal skill. You are able to stand up for yourself. However, if you answered no, then you must reflect on what your points of weakness are and learn to strengthen them.

Chapter 9 – Cooperation and Collaboration Skills: There is No "I" in Team

While we aim to improve ourselves, we should, however, take into consideration that other people are significant parts of who we are as a person. Being a team player is an indicative element in improving interpersonal skills.

At home, you can work on your cooperation skills better when you take part in house chores or in the payment of bills. You can also work on this certain skill when you join family outings despite your busy schedule.

In school, some students struggle with working on this particular skill because they are trained to be competitive. However, students must know that being able to work with others would be a good training ground for them in the future, as they will have colleagues to work with as well. Although it is alright to be competitive, students must always keep it to a minimal and healthy level. If students, at an early age, are not taught to work effectively with other people, they will end up being selfish and inconsiderate. The said traits are neither admirable nor helpful at working environments. Thus, at an early age, they must learn how to cooperate and collaborate with others.

As they say, no matter how excellent you are as a professional, if you do not get along with your colleagues, you will not get far. Same as in the school setting, workers who do not get along with others are not favored upon by their employers. To avoid this, reach out and work well with your co-workers.

Do not delay work, especially when others are depending upon you. Lend a helping hand to those who have too much workload, or just ask how their weekend went. It is important that you maintain a healthy working relationship and through these interpersonal skills, you can achieve that.

With this interpersonal skill, you should be able to ask yourself this question: "Do I work with others well or would I rather work alone?" While there is nothing wrong with being able to work on your own, it is still necessary that you are capable of working with others. If you find it difficult to cooperate in groups, then you should work on this certain interpersonal skill more.

Chapter 10 – Problem Solving Skills: Working with Grace under Pressure

Problems are part of our daily lives. There will always be situations that will push us to our limits. This is normal. Feeling pressured about these situations is also normal. Everyone feels countless anxieties brought about by the fear of not meeting deadlines or not being able to solve a particular problem.

However, it should be remembered that a person who has excellent interpersonal skills handles his stresses better and more effectively. While no one can provide ways to remove stress (as this is impossible!), there are, however, ways on how you can deal with them without losing your poise (and your mind!).

1. Once you are faced with a challenge, it is always best to take a deep breath and assess the situation first. Identify the problem. At first glance, people can already study whether a particular task is easy or difficult for them. Just by evaluating the situation, you will already know if this task requires extra effort on your part. Study the situation and dissect the problem. After identifying your problem, make sure you fully understand it so that you can prepare a thorough solution.

2. Once you know what the problem is, study all your possible options. Once they have identified their problem, some people become so occupied with the problem's gravity that their minds are clouded by how difficult it is. Avoid this mindset, as this will hinder you from formulating all your options.

Open your mind to different choices. When faced with problems, try to come up with at least three solutions so that you always have a contingency plan, just in case one does not work. Be sure to exhaust all possible situations.

3. Organize your thoughts and strategize. When you have a list of options in your hand, the next thing you should do is create a game plan according to each option. Prioritize which option has the greater chance of delivering results and then strategize.

4. Ask for help, if you must. There is nothing wrong with asking others for assistance. In your strategizing phase, it is evident that there are still things that you may have missed or have failed to consider, but could be greatly helpful in solving your problem. Other people may find this loophole for you. In addition, there are situations when your problem is not exactly your field of expertise and you would need someone to help you understand.

Being able to solve your problems efficiently and effectively is important in developing your interpersonal skills because it homes you into a socially mature person.

When assessing your problem solving skills, the question you should ask yourself is this: "Do I face my problems maturely and competently?" People who find solutions to their problems are competent while those who focus on their hardships lack the willpower to strengthen this interpersonal skill. If you are able to face your problems with possible solutions without breaking down, then your problem solving skills are well developed.

Chapter 11 – Self Management Skills: The Personal in Interpersonal

Now that you know how to communicate well with people using your different interpersonal skills, it is time to know how you can develop the last, but definitely not the least interpersonal skill you have. Self-management skills deal with how you control yourself, particularly your emotions, when faced with certain situations or surroundings.

Countless scenarios trigger different emotions within us and some of these situations are very difficult to manage. However, this is where your self-management skills come in. In every situation that affects a person, there is a corresponding reaction. However, not every behavior is deemed appropriate.

We all go through bad days. There will be days when we feel like we can take over the world despite our obstacles. There will be days when we feel like giving up. Some days are just terrible. Your car broke down while you were hurrying to work or you lost a competition, which you trained so hard for. On days when you feel down, always remember that you may not have control over the situation you are in, but you are in control of your emotions. So take a deep breath and calm down.

Whenever you come across difficult situations, you will always have that inclination to give up. As humans, we let our emotions get the best of us. However, this is neither advisable nor healthy. When dealing with negative emotions such as anger, frustration or sadness, you should always try to relax first and assess the situation. Contrary to what you may think at the time, no scenario is ever hopeless. There is always a way – and that way does not have anything to do with getting angry or crying.

1. The first thing you have to do is to relax. Think of happy and positive thoughts to help you get by, even if it is only for a few minutes. When you let your mind wander off from the situation or from the problem for a little while, it gives you a sense of relief and it helps you take in the problem more clearly and effectively.

2. Ponder on the brighter side of things. There are times when a situation is too difficult that the solution does not happen right away. Try to keep yourself sane by trying to make the best out of every situation. A single problem does not mean it is the end of everything so focus on that thought and work on other aspects of your life.

    If you are having problems at work, try to think how blessed you are when it comes to your family and friends. If you are having marital problems, try to ponder on the good aspects of your life, like your career or your children. Always try to be positive, even if it is challenging to do.

3. Lastly, when you come across problems, always remind yourself that emotionally unstable people are taxing to be with. You do not want to be the kind of person everyone avoids because they see you as stressful. When you realize this particular fact, you will stop indulging in your worries.

By maintaining proper behavior and conduct, you will become a better person because you get to handle your situations well. You are mature enough to accept the difficulties in life and you are strong enough to solve them without surrendering.

The question to ask yourself when assessing your self-management skill is this: "Do I control my emotions or do I let them control me?" People who do not let their worries take over them are emotionally stable, very self-confident and end up forming better personal and professional relationships.

Conclusion

Thank you again for purchasing this guide.

If you enjoyed this guide, please take the time to share your thoughts and post a review. It'd be greatly appreciated!

Thank you and good luck!